T0365799

THE GOLD MINE

What Would You Do?

Deane Addison Knapp

AuthorHouse™ LLC
1663 Liberty Drive
Bloomington, IN 47403
www.authorhouse.com
Phone: 1-800-839-8640

© 2014 Deane Addison Knapp. All rights reserved.

No part of this book may be reproduced, stored in a retrieval system,
or transmitted by any means without the written permission of the author.

Published by AuthorHouse: 09/04/2014

ISBN: 978-1-4969-3764-3 (sc)
*   978-1-4969-3765-0 (e)*

Library of Congress Control Number: 2014915777

Printed in the United States of America

This book is printed on acid-free paper.

Because of the dynamic nature of the Internet, any web addresses or links contained in this book may have
changed since publication and may no longer be valid. The views expressed in this work are solely those
of the author and do not necessarily reflect the views of the publisher, and the publisher hereby disclaims
any responsibility for them.

In this you greatly rejoice, though now for a little while you may have had to suffer grief in all kinds of trials. These have come so that your faith---of greater worth than gold---may be proved genuine...

Peter

Before this faith came, we were held prisoner by the law, locked up until faith should be revealed. So the law was put in charge to lead us to Christ that we might be justified by faith. Now that faith has come, we are no longer under the supervision of the law.

Paul

I am the Lord's servant. May it be to me as you have said.

Mary

The thief comes only to steal and kill and destroy; I have come that they may have life, and have it to the full.

Jesus

THE GOLD MINE

INTRODUCTION

A gold mine is supposed to have gold in it. Most don't have very much. But if it has any at all, it's still called a gold mine.

Potential. No gold mine has ever been started that didn't have potential. Most gold mines have more potential than gold.

Prospectors. Most prospectors, who have a gold mine with potential, know what to do: dig. Most prospectors, who find way more gold than their mine's potential, don't know what to do.

One curiously asks himself: What kind of prospector am I? What kind of gold mine do I have?

A person, young or old, has to be an optimist, and have hope, some would say faith, to continue to dig in a mine whose greatest asset is potential.

1

The years had been hard. The digging had been hard. But every time a vein of a few inches had shown up, it whetted the appetite. It hoped of much, much more. The potential was for much, much more. It just took digging, and lots of it.

Juan was digging in California, in a mine that had been started by a distant relative long ago. The person had died in the mine and a long line of relatives had passed on it, as an inheritance, until Juan. He decided he could work hard, since there was the potential for gold, even though the curse on the mine, because of the death, was there, too.

Day after day, year after year he would leave his small ranch and walk up into the hills to his mine. His faithful wife and five children would be there every evening when he came back, eager to see if there was a smile on his face, a smile that spoke more of gold than potential.

They all knew of the curse, but did not think about it. If the curse became a reality before the potential did, all would be lost. Possibly a life, the meager ranch, and all of the potential their lives were holding onto. Juan was brave, Juan was courageous, and Juan was patient and persistent, but only God knew the future. Would God bless with untold riches, or would he bless with disaster, in order to make them stronger, more able to trust Him in life? These were his thoughts.

Every day Juan would ask himself these questions. He would say a prayer each morning before entering the mine. Safety for his family, safety for himself, and a rich reward for his hard work, with the exception of His will for their lives, no matter what, as Jesus had prayed.

Not knowing the future gave Juan a fifty/fifty chance. If disaster was coming... well, he refused to think about it. In his mind, seeing disaster as a blessing did not ever work. But, that was God's business, not his. His was to dig. Dig and simply believe. After all, God knew what He was doing.

And so he would dig and pray. Pray and dig. He did not want to artificially influence God toward the blessing of riches if he and his family were not ready to handle it. God saw through things like that. On the other hand he did not want to be behind in asking. Jesus said whatever Juan asked according to His will would be granted him.

Every time Juan would find a small vein, enough to live on for a month or two, he would be thankful, appropriately so, for the blessing. But he would wonder if the other side of the equation would be next. With a fifty/fifty chance, you couldn't have blessing piled upon blessing without disaster mounting up. Should he quit while he was ahead and find other work, or were true riches just beyond where he was?

The blessing of riches took hard work; the blessing of disaster struck suddenly with unknown consequences. Juan did not understand that part. But that was God's business. His was to accept, and say thank you.

What about the curse? How did that fit in? Was the curse under God's overall authority? Did the blessings of riches just enrage the curse and make it stronger? Did the curse join with God's blessing of disaster when hardship was called for in Juan's life?

What hard decisions God had to make. Just believe, Juan. Just believe.

2

One day Juan was digging fifty feet in, at the end of the mine, and his pick hit the rock with a slightly different sound. He stopped and put down his pick. That was the sound he was always listening for.

In the light of his lantern, Juan picked up his small shovel and carefully wiggled it into the cracked rocks and pried gently. The rock crumbled and fell to the ground. He saw gold.

Not knowing if it was a small vein or a larger one, he controlled his excitement. If he got too excited, more than his love for God excited him, God could instantly make the vein smaller. From experience, Juan knew that his love for God was more important to God, than Juan's need for gold. He carefully reached down for his lantern and held it up to the shiny area. It was gold. He had hit gold.

The area Juan had uncovered looked very promising. But he held his emotions in check and began to express thanksgiving to God for answering his prayers. He was safe, hopefully his family was safe, and God had rewarded his hard work. Juan desperately wanted to chip another shovelful away from the area, but he quickly repressed the thought and forced his mind to recount whatever else had happened that he could say "thank you" for.

Juan had to be careful, this was serious business. God could increase or decrease the size of the find according to how Juan acted. Better to go slowly and show the wisdom he had amassed over the years of near fruitless digging. Whatever happened, it would be an expression of God's love for him; Juan knew this. But the fact that he was tired of working hard for very little reward kept wanting to surface, and he could not let it. One wrong move at this junction could mean years of more hard work.

Juan took a deep breath and, staring at the gold, began trying to recall if he had not forgiven anyone, sincerely from his heart. "Lord," he said out loud, "I really want to do this right. You know my heart and what I am capable of doing wrong. I submit my will to you, and thankfully receive from your hand whatever you decide." Okay so far; the gold was still there, looking better than ever.

Juan decided to sit down on his small stool. He put the lantern on the ground. It still showed off some of the gleam of the gold. He decided to just sit and enjoy the moment. He was at the tipping point, rich reward or hard work. Not knowing was not a bad place. It still had hope, still had faith, it still had potential. He wanted to rest for a while, in the realm of faith, before reality hit.

As he sat, he began to wonder how long he could balance at this spot. Could he hold off untold riches or more hard work, whichever it was, to give himself time to go over his life and make amends?

It would be trying to influence God's decision, but not for greed. He wanted his family to prosper. They depended on him and could not provide wealth for themselves. He could. That is, God could. And oh, the proud feelings his family would have for him if he produced. They deserved that, even though he didn't. Every family needs a time to be proud of their father and husband.

Juan focused on the gold again. It was still there.

Juan's feelings tried to erupt again. He caught them and gathered them in. Yelling and screaming and jumping for joy would definitely not be the thing to do until the facts were fully known. Then God couldn't change things without it being a visible miracle.

What if he just left it, and went home, unexcited, and proved to God and everyone, he was ready? He was ready to handle riches, without his love and commitment for God dwindling. Or, what if he just stayed here and sat on his stool, keeping an eye on his find? His wife would finally come to find out why he was late and she could bring him back some food. Or, what if he just busted out all over, yelling and screaming down to the house and into town to the bar and got drunk with celebration?

What would happen depended on what he did.

3

Juan approached the little ranch slowly. He walked up onto the porch carefully, keeping his emotions corralled and his mind busy. What else could he be thankful for, and what else needed to be forgiven?

The trouble was, he would be thankful and then forget and naturally start grumbling about things, especially how hard his work was. He would forgive, from the heart, and then later remember the hurt and think badly about someone again. It was a difficult maneuver to constantly check what he was thinking and feeling, and try to correct it. And God was always watching, because he never slept. Not that God was mean, He just knew what was best for him and his family. Juan's job was to yield to His will no matter what, as Jesus had done.

"Hi Honey, how is everyone?" Juan was a little more self-assured than usual because he had seen gold with his own eyes.

"We're all good, my dear husband; you…look like you have something on your mind, how did today go?" Bernice could read him like a book.

"My day went well as usual, with a small exception on the good side." Juan began. Bernice had kissed him on the cheek while wiping a plate with a dish cloth. She stopped wiping as he continued, "I'd like to go into town tomorrow, just you and me. Do you think we could do that?"

Bernice finished with the plate and put it away, hung the dish cloth on the rack, and wiped her hands on her apron. "Yes, that would be fun. What would we do?"

"Oh, I have a number of things in mind, so we might as well start early. Can the kids be alone for the day?

"Yes, they will be fine. I'll go get them into bed, and you eat your dinner. Then we'll read them a story and tell them about tomorrow together." Bernice knew something was up, but did not want to spoil her husband's plans by asking too many questions.

So far, so good; faith was being assured without seeing. Juan had seen, but only partially. Believing God for His blessing, riches or more labor, which ever it would turn out to be, was still faith, because he wisely had not uncovered any more of the find. This walking with God was a delicate walk of balance, but so far he had not fallen, and faith is what pleases God.

Dinner, a story, then family prayers and kisses took place. Tomorrow they would bring home something special for the kids. "Remember your chores and remember

God is always watching and protecting. We'll be home for dinner. Good night my dear children."

The little ranch was at peace through the night. Juan fell asleep wondering if anything was happening up at the end of the mine.

4

Morning came with sunshine. Juan and Bernice dressed, ate breakfast, and readied the horse and buggy. They went back in and kissed the children and left a note of instruction. As they were leaving, Juan stopped in the kitchen and took the savings can off the top shelf. He emptied it all into a small leather pouch. Bernice just watched in case there might be an explanation. Juan, she could see had plans.

On the trip into town, Juan began mapping out what he wanted to do.

"I want to stop at the Caldwell's and see how John's wife's recovery is going. Then stop at the church and put two dollars in the poor box."

About an hour later, when those two things were checked off to Juan's satisfaction, they moved up the street to the General Store. First thing Juan did was pay off their debt. He put ten dollars extra on the account, and then they shopped a bit.

Bernice knew something was up but resigned herself to enjoying shopping as if paying for it was not her concern. She would believe in her husband, he would sense it, and be proud that he was doing his job. Reality would have to wait, along with her plans for the savings.

They had lunch in the hotel's dining room. This was only the third time in their twelve years of marriage that they had dined out. It was heavenly not to cook and not to clean up, but it cost five dollars because they had dessert also.

The buggy got dropped off at the livery stable and had a thorough going over by the attendant, and the horse got new shoes. Meanwhile, Juan took Bernice's hand and strolled up the street to the assayer's office to make a personal, private appointment two days hence. Then the bank, where Juan and Bernice opened an account with five dollars, half of what remained in the pouch.

Money for birthdays, Christmas, and winter food was now gone. Bernice wondered and hoped, and believed in her husband; she decided to help make this the best day possible. It might not happen again for a while. Unless...no stop...no unless. Her hopes couldn't handle another rising and abrupt fall. Her desires had been dashed too many times. But she was thankful it was getting easier to submit her will to the will of God. She had very little will left.

Bernice clung to her husband's arm and went with him into the hardware store. Juan bought new tools, one for each of the children, to brighten their thoughts about working around the ranch. He was a loving father, a good father, and she was blessed to have him.

They picked up the buggy and horse, and had a couple bales of hay loaded. Juan gave the last fifty cents to the attendant as a tip. The trip home was peaceful, for Juan. He had accomplished all he wanted to do. Bernice was simply there, as his wife, his dear wife.

As soon as they got home, Juan laid out the new tools. Each child was given the appropriate one. They marveled at them and put them in their right place for tomorrow's work. The two older ones took care of the horse and buggy and hay. The younger ones showed their mom what they were preparing for dinner. As life returned to normal after the trip into town and a wonderful dinner, Juan pulled out candy and new reading books and settled the children down.

Then he said to Bernice, "Walk up to the mine with me. We still have an hour of daylight left."

She changed into her walking shoes, grasped her husband's arm and off they went.

5

Juan took each step with peace. He had addressed each accusation in his mind and now approached the mine with confidence. He would be able to face whatever was there, knowing he had done everything required of him, that is, at least everything that had come to mind.

At the entrance to the mine he stopped and addressed Bernice. "Honey, I want to show you what I found yesterday."

"Tell me about it first, dear." Bernice had to have her heart prepared. She could not over guess, it would be a nightmare.

"No, my love, just come see." Juan picked up the lantern, lit it and proceeded into the mine followed by his wife. Even at this point, he could not describe to her what he had found. It might have changed. He would let her see it as he had seen it, then they could go from there. This delicate balance of walking with God was his gift to his wife and his family. God would be pleased; not impressed, but pleased. He was walking by faith, not by sight.

The silence of the mine, with only the echo of their footsteps was eerie to Bernice. She was not used to it. It had an odd chill, too, but they continued and Juan slowed as they came to the end of his digging. He raised the lantern and drew his wife to his side.

The brilliant gleam of the gold he had uncovered yesterday was still there. But something was different. Some more rock had fallen off, and more gold showed. Juan stared and was stunned. He had carefully walked the right course in his thinking, saying, and doing, and God had rewarded him. The hand of God had uncovered more gold. "Do you see it, my dear wife?"

"Yes, my dear husband. I see beautiful shiny gold. Tell me about what I am seeing!"

Juan felt for the stool with his foot and sat his wife down on it. "This is more than I saw yesterday. The hand of God has taken away more rock. He has smiled at our humble approach to his blessing and revealed more. It is so beautiful."

"Yes. It is very beautiful. Shall we pick at it some more? It looks like it continues."

"No! We must not. He has rewarded us for our submission to his overall will and our greater love for him than for riches. We must not turn aside from that, but continue on. Do you understand my dear wife? When we act according to His will He rewards us. We do not want to fall off one way or the other."

Bernice looked at her husband. He knew God so well. Juan was a gift from God to her. Now her husband had been given a gift for all his hard work, and for the effect it had worked in his heart over the years. "I wonder how far it goes?"

"It goes as far as He chooses to enrich us. It is His plan, His will, not ours." Juan felt like just staying and watching it all night. Oh, to see another chunk of rock fall away without his hand doing it. Suddenly he felt like he was leaning too far to one side. "Come my love. What we can see with our eyes will not disappear. We will come back tomorrow and see what else God has done."

6

The wonderful sleep Bernice and Juan both had, they were convinced, was God's favor. It was undeserved of course, although it wouldn't have come without their delicately balanced walk. They breakfasted together as a family and then, as the children attended to their chores, Bernice and Juan headed for the mine.

It was hard not to go fast, but they busied themselves with reciting memorized Bible verses. It calmed them to know that what they had seen yesterday could not be taken away.

At the mine they stopped and Juan said the prayers he said every morning before entering. It was nice to have his wife with him. Juan could feel the curse backing off as they walked into the mine with prayers leading the way. "Oh Lord, I will walk with your balance again today."

The lantern showed the golden gleam at the end of the tunnel. It was the same as yesterday. Juan took his small leather pouch out of his pocket and handed it to Bernice. He took his small shovel and approached the gold with reverent care. With a few minutes of work, he dug out a small nugget of gold. He held it in his hand for a while, and then handed it to his wife to hold and put into the pouch. This being done, he looked at the area of gold in the light of the lantern and had the strong desire to dig some more rock away. He felt God's peace and decided to do it.

Juan handed the lantern to Bernice and took a deep breath and said to her, "I'm going to dig a little. It's what I do every day, so I feel it will be alright to do." He did not know whether to dig up, over, or down, so he said a silent prayer and started at the top of the gold, going up toward God. He worked his shovel precisely and skillfully, and a large amount of rubble crumbled to the floor of the gold mine.

Bernice held the lantern up higher and the new area showed more gold. Juan moved the lantern down to see the crumbled rocks and saw no chunks of gold had fallen. He took a deep breath. Now what? Juan dared to reach his hand up and place his palm on the gold. But no, that would be too much. He held his hand an inch away, as if blessing the gold. Yes. "I bless you in Jesus' name." Juan said this out loud and felt wonderful for doing it. Ok, step by step he was walking with God.

"It's beautiful." Bernice said with less excitement than she felt.

"Yes it is. Come dear wife, let's go back home." And with that, Juan took Bernice's hand, and walked out of the mine.

7

Juan's family had a wonderful rest of the day. They worked together on weeding the small plots of crops and the big area of the vegetable garden, which was Bernice's domain. She tended it and had say over what happened there.

Dinner was chicken soup, cornbread, and apple pie. The children felt like the family was celebrating something, with the good food, and the special things their dad and mom had brought back from town. So they enjoyed it, did their evening chores, their bedtime routine, and snuggled safe and warm into their beds. Dad and Mom were taking another trip into town tomorrow and they couldn't wait to see what they would bring back this time.

As before, Juan and Bernice left early and arrived at the assayer's office at their appointed time. Juan shook hands with the officer and dug out the small leather pouch from his pocket. He poured the contents onto the tray so the assayer could test the quality of the gold.

Mr. Martin had been acquainted with Juan and Beatrice for years, testing the small portions of gold they brought in occasionally. He now stared at the chunk on the tray. It was larger than he had seen in a while. He carefully measured it four different ways and then put it on the scale to weigh. He wrote in his book the weight and measurements and then put on his magnifying eyepiece.

Mr. Martin took fully a minute to look from many different angles. He finally put down the chunk and his eyepiece and looked first into Juan's eyes, and then Bernice's. Then he said, "Please sit down," as he walked around them to the front door and locked it.

"Where did you get this gold, Juan?"

"From our mine, sir"

"I doubt this chunk came from the same mine from which you have always brought samples to me."

"Yes sir, the same mine."

"Juan, this chunk is pure gold. Gold does not come out of the ground this way around here. It has to be refined, just like the samples you always bring in. The only way to have pure gold that looks like this chunk is to take some gold coins and melt and reshape them into a rough looking chunk, like this one."

Mr. Martin waited for Juan's reply, but seeing the blank look on his face, he continued in a softer voice. "Juan, the only reason to do that would be because the coins had been stolen."

Mr. Martin waited again, but still no reply. "Juan, we are friends. Tell me what you've done and I will help you straighten it out."

Bernice lifted her hand and placed it on her husband's arm. Juan had his mouth open but nothing was coming out.

"Sir," Bernice started, "we both saw the gold at the end of the mine about waist high to shoulder high. We…didn't uncover more of it because…" She hesitated.

"Because why, Bernice?"

"Because…we didn't…know what to do."

"…so we gouged a chunk out…and brought it to you." Juan finished for his wife. He had never been accused of stealing before and knew he was innocent.

Mr. Martin looked both of them in the eye again and then looked down at the chunk. "Okay folks. The law in this case requires me to report this to the Sheriff. I must do that. But I will bring him with me to your house and the four of us will go see what you found at the end of your mine."

"Thank you sir, we will be at home waiting for you. Will you come today?"

"Yes, Juan. We will be there this afternoon." Mr. Martin hesitated and then said. "Juan, I need to keep this chunk as evidence. I will write out a receipt for you, if you want, but if this goes to court, the receipt will prove I got this chunk from you."

"Please, Mr. Martin, I'd like a receipt." Juan and Bernice were holding hands.

"Alright then," Mr. Martin wrote out the receipt and handed it to Juan and Bernice to sign. "Folks, I choose to believe you, but I must obey the law."

"Yes sir, thank you." The couple rose to leave as Mr. Martin unlocked the door. Ushering them out, he closed the door and looked down shaking his head.

Juan and Bernice sat huddled together in the buggy on the way home. They spoke just above the sound of travel. The exhilaration they had held back was still there, because the gold was still there. But being accused, even falsely, was unsettling.

Or was the gold still there? Would God take it away? If it was not there for the two men to see, the accusation against them would be stronger. Juan knew he was a wicked man. There was a lot of work God still needed to do in his heart. However, he would not be able to bear this. He could feel the doubt and fear. Would God allow him to be taken away from his family and thrown into jail, even though falsely accused, just to get at the wickedness he had been afraid to have God deal with?

The gold had to be there. It just had to be. They had seen it with their own eyes. God could not take that away. As they made their way home, they wanted to run up and check the mine.

"No," Juan said, "it would not be right." There was no room for doubt and fear in this scenario. The gold was there, pure gold. They had seen it. He smiled at his wife. They were standing on the rock of truth. And on that rock I will build my family, Jesus had said. They rode on in peace, balanced. Trying to believe and not be afraid.

8

The children were expecting their folks any minute. They had enjoyed working with their new tools and morning chores were done. Lunch was being prepared, leftovers of course. Lunch was always leftovers.

As the buggy came through the big gate down by the road, the children ran out of the house waving. It was then that the earth began to shake. The children felt it first and the oldest corralled the rest together. Juan and Bernice didn't know what the odd feeling was until the intensity increased. Juan pulled the buggy to a stop beside the children and they jumped down and joined them. By the time they were all huddled together, it had stopped. As they looked around, dust and dirt were settling. They looked each other over carefully, and then at the house. It all looked normal except for the swirling dust. Juan busied his family checking the house, barns and livestock.

The Sheriff and Mr. Martin were on horseback and felt the shuddering right away. Knowing where they were going, they looked at each other with astonishment. Mines were known to collapse in earthquakes. If this had happened an hour later, they very well could have been trapped or crushed.

The Sheriff began to count in his mind how many mines were in the area. It was the middle of the day. Miners had to have been mining. He spurred his horse into a gallop and they soon arrived at Juan's ranch.

Lunch was being served, and travelers never said no to lunch.

As they sat down to eat, the Sheriff formulated his questions. "Juan, how long ago did you find the gold?" He asked conversationally, between mouthfuls.

"Ah…four days ago, sir." Juan wanted to make sure his answer was correct.

"And you found a lot of it?"

"Yes sir."

"So how come nobody in town has heard about it? It must have excited you."

Juan paused at a very good question. How would he explain his careful walk with God. "Yes sir…it did excite me…but I…I knew it would be the wrong thing to do to get all excited first off. There would be plenty of time for that."

"How much do you think you found?"

"I have no idea. I only uncovered enough to see it and take a sample for Mr. Martin to look at."

"Has anyone else seen it?"

"Yes sir, I showed it to my wife the next day."

The Sheriff looked at Bernice, "Real good lunch ma'am. You must have been excited, too, when you saw the gold. What did it look like?"

"Well, it was shiny, gleaming gold, and…"

Juan interrupted his wife. "Why don't we just show you, Sheriff?"

"Alright." The Sheriff said wiping his mouth with the red and white checkered cloth by his plate. "Let's just do that."

The four walked up to the mine and noticed dust had settled on everything around the entrance.

"Sure glad you weren't in the mine when the quake hit." The Sheriff offered.

"Yes sir, thank you. I'm sure glad we all weren't in it." Juan said as they approached the mine. The little shack with Juan's tools in it was intact. He grabbed two lanterns and they entered the mine, carefully.

Bernice held her apron up to her nose and mouth as the men did with their handkerchiefs. All along the fifty feet of mine, rocks had crumbled to the floor. A few big piles had fallen from the ceiling and the group had to step over or around them.

Juan was counting his steps so if there was a blockage, he would know how far from the end they were. With ten feet to go they encountered solid rubble, from floor to ceiling.

"Is this the end, Juan?"

"No sir. Ten more feet."

"Which way?"

"Straight into the rubble."

The Sheriff stepped up level with Juan. He took the lantern from Juan and surveyed the rubble, walls, floor and ceiling. "Martin," he said.

Mr. Martin came up and looked also. "Yes, I'd say it had been dug out and collapsed back in. How far do you figure, Juan?"

"Ten feet, right about."

"Ok," said the Sheriff, "let's head back out."

Out at the entrance they stood in a circle for a minute breathing fresh air. The Sheriff spoke, "About two weeks ago, someone stole a sack of gold coins from the railroad car that carried the payroll to the big mine up at the end of the valley. We figure it was just one person because there were a lot of sacks and only one was missing. The train stopped in town to load supplies, water and wood. It was the last stop and the money was apparently all there when the train left town, but gone when it arrived up at the end of the valley. Then when you showed up with that gold, Juan, two and two equaled four. Now I'm going to give you the benefit of the doubt, but I want to come up here in one week and see the end of this mine. Are we square on that?"

Juan thought for a moment. "Yes sir, I'll get right on it."

"Well now, be careful. I'm not saying kill yourself. We could have aftershocks, more cave-ins. You know what to do." The Sheriff turned to Bernice and removed his hat and said, "Sure appreciate the hospitality ma'am. I'm going to tell my wife about your apple pie. Good afternoon all." The Sheriff and Mr. Martin headed back down to the ranch and their horses. They had been watered and groomed, and fed a few apples. The men mounted their horses and then the Sheriff looked at the children, "If I need to form up a posse in the future, would you kids be willing to be deputized?"

"Yes sir." They all yelled. The two men and their horses were gone in a cloud of dust.

9

Juan and Bernice watched the two men go, and then gazed at each other. What in the world was going on?

The gold was real. They had seen it, looked at it, and touched it. Well, almost touched it. The small chunk they had touched. They were sure, without one doubt that it was there. Yet they were the only ones in the whole world who were sure it was there.

It was the curse. The curse had caused the earth to shake and the mine to partially collapse. Juan's careful balanced walk had kept it from harming anyone. His prayers and actions had made a difference. In fact, the mine could have completely collapsed, but no, only ten feet. And how much more of the gold would be uncovered when he got to it?

God's hand of blessing had moved again; more hard work, but with definite riches at the end. Somehow the curse, Juan, and God, were wrapped up in a struggle of good versus evil. And God couldn't bless with only riches until the curse was gone.

The reality of the gold stayed with Juan all week. It affected his mind, taking the place of his fear for the future. No more fifty/fifty. True riches had moved into the realm of reality, with just a little more hard work. Now when things went wrong he remembered the mine and its contents with its 100% purity, and peace and joy were returned. Juan had tentatively dealt with the doubt and fear. But how was he to get rid of the curse?

One of his distant relatives had died in the mine. Juan wasn't sure of the circumstances or the exact date, but the curse of this death went with the mine. The relative must have done something wrong. Curses don't just show up for no reason. Whatever that wrong was it had opened the door for the curse, which then caused the death. If whatever he had done wrong could be righted, no more curse. Then, with no more curse, no more fifty/fifty blessings. It would be a 100% blessing of riches, because Juan knew the gold was there.

So, how do you right a wrong?

Juan had no idea, except that his balanced walk with God was helping. His prayers and his walk were keeping him safe while he worked. It was his mind that he had trouble controlling. His speech and his actions were hard enough to control, but he was doing it. It was the thoughts that snuck up on him…from his evil heart…they were not helpful.

If a wrong done by the one who owned the mine, who was also the one who died, invited in the curse, could a right done by the new owner, who was still alive, satisfy the curse? This was a little above Juan's ability to comprehend. If he dug out the mine, and took some of the gold and used it to fund a community park, or even build a church building, would that get rid of the curse?

Of course his balanced walk with God would have to keep him safe until this all could happen, but it was something he could do. But then, if he became wealthy, blessing others was something he would do anyway, curse or no curse.

His only option was to do what he knew to do. And that was dig.

10

Praying, walking carefully, and digging brought Juan to the sixth day of work since the Sheriff's visit. There had been no aftershocks, no more cave-ins, and so far, no gold.

Juan had put a mark on the wall where he had started to dig out the rubble, and he had gone ten feet. Doubts had begun to creep back into his mind this morning, but he said "no" to them as soon as he caught himself.

At noon, Juan walked down to the house for some lunch. When he got back an hour later, he stopped before entering and said a prayer. "God, if I'm not doing the right thing, just show me. Show me what to do and I'll do it." Then he lit his lantern and walked the fifty feet.

As he neared the end, his light began picking up something shiny. Juan's eyes got big, as he held the lantern up. More rock had fallen away while he had been gone to lunch, and there was the gold.

Juan didn't move. He was afraid to. God's hand had moved, but how did it relate to what he had done or not done. Juan suddenly felt something was wrong. He turned and quickly got out of the mine.

Outside the entrance he sat down and went over things. His speech and actions were good, but his mind was still giving him trouble. Yet God had moved the rubble away to reveal the gold while Juan was gone. It was a reward for his trying, but he had to be very careful. He walked back down to the house and summoned Bernice, and hand in hand they walked back to the mine.

"Pray with me." Juan said and they sat and prayed together at the entrance.

Then Juan said, "Stay here and continue to pray. I want to look again." Into the mine he went. When he got to the end, the gold was still there. Juan carefully shoveled a wheelbarrow full of rubble and wheeled it out. As usual, he sifted through it before and after he dumped it onto the rubble pile. "If you will keep praying I will get one more load of rubble, then we'll both go back and have a look."

Bernice liked being a precise part of the work of receiving their riches. She prayed earnestly.

Juan, shoveling another load, but carefully not looking at the gold, returned with a more peaceful countenance. He talked as he sifted. "God caused more rubble to fall, I have removed it, you are praying, and the gold is there, larger than ever. Come on, let's go see together."

Bernice was shaking her head with a growing smile. They did not know what to do. Touch it or not touch it. Dig more or not dig more. Not being able to see the end or sides of the vein, they could not calculate its amount. It was big and seemed to continue in all directions. The height, the width, the length, or the depth was not measureable.

Then Juan had a thought and it was just too strong of an urge to hold back. He took the small leather pouch out of his pocket and handed it to Bernice. With his small shovel he picked at the center of the gold and dug enough out to fill the pouch to the top. Then they left the mine as carefully and as quickly as they could.

Bernice held on to her husband's arm as they walked silently down to the house. Inside, Juan took the empty savings can off the high shelf and put the pouch full of gold in it. Putting it back, he turned to his wife and they hugged.

That night the family had fun together, as usual, but it seemed to be easier. Bernice and Juan kept glancing at the top shelf and grins broke out on their faces. They just couldn't help it.

Then it was bed time. Tomorrow they were expecting the Sheriff and Mr. Martin for lunch again.

11

In the middle of the night sometime, Juan had a dream. In his dream, he had gotten up on a regular workday and left for the mine. But by the time he had gotten to the mine, he was so tired all he could do was sit. Meanwhile, worker after worker came out of the mine with loads of pure gold. They loaded it onto pack horses which had the name of the bank stenciled on the big canvas bags. His gold was going down to the bank and into his account without him lifting a hand. When the day was over he hobbled back to the house and by the time he got there, he felt fine.

When Juan woke up the next morning, he remembered the dream. He got up and told his wife he was running up to the mine just to check it, and would be back for breakfast. The first thing he did was to take the can off the top shelf and make sure the gold was still there. Then out he went.

When he got to the mine he felt fine. With lantern in hand, he walked to the end. Nothing had changed. That feeling came over Juan again and he dug more gold out of the center of the vein, enough to fill his pockets.

Back down to the house, he rummaged around till he found another can. He put the gold in it. Now there were two cans full on the top shelf.

As soon as breakfast was out of the way, Bernice and the younger ones began preparing for lunch, including apple pie. Juan helped the older ones with chores and soon the whole ranch was ship-shape for company.

When their guests from town came through the gate just after noon, they all were ready. The older children quickly took care of the two big horses and soon all were sat down to lunch.

"Well now, folks," the Sheriff started out after grace was said, "Martin here and I are chomping at the bit to see what you found in your mine. The lost bag of gold coins I told you about last week was found. Well, sort of. Those darn bankers deal with lots of big numbers, but can't count to twenty-five accurately enough to save their lives. They never did lose it, and just got around to telling me about it two days ago." The Sheriff stopped to take another bite, but wasn't finished. "I do apologize for falsely accusing you both of stealing. It comes with the job, once in a while, to be wrong."

Bernice started the plates of food around again. "Don't bother to leave room for dessert, Sheriff. I know you don't much care for my apple pie."

"Oh, good Lord. Martin, we got to find reason to come up this way more often."

"Well, be careful what you wish for, Sheriff. If there's any amount of gold up in that mine like the chunk I laid eyes on last week, they're going to need an armed escort to bring it to town. I told Manning, at the bank, to start building a bigger vault and I wasn't half kidding."

Everyone was in a good mood and when the plates were being removed and dessert served, Mr. Martin remembered part of what he was there for. He dug in his pocket and put forty-five dollars on the table. "Here, this is what the chunk of gold you gave me last week weighed out at: forty-four dollars and fifty-five cents. I just rounded it up to forty five dollars even, to make myself feel better about thinking you had stolen it, Juan."

Bernice and Juan smiled at each other. This was like Christmas and it had only begun.

As the four ambled up to the mine on full stomachs, Juan asked the Sheriff what he knew about the death which had occurred in the mine.

"Well, not much. It was before my time. The person that died apparently was not murdered, not killed by an accident in the mine, and too young to die of old age. Some say he died of a broken heart. Either because of a woman, I suppose, or not finding any gold."

"Did the man have any record of wrong doing or prison?"

"Not that I ever heard. He was a relative of yours wasn't he?"

"Yes, some sort of relative. One I never knew."

When the lanterns were lit, the party entered the mine. Being basically a hole burrowed into the earth, it was dank and dark with a chill, the lanterns the only light.

At the end it was crowded, so Juan, having led the way , now let the Sheriff and Mr. Martin step up to look. The assayer looked as the Sheriff held up the lantern. He put his eye piece on and went close. He inspected at the middle, then at the top, bottom and sides of the wall. He took out a small tool and picked a chunk out of the gold. He weighed it in his hand, smelled it and licked it with his tongue. Then he stepped back and the Sheriff moved in. He put his palm on the wall in four different places and then shook his head and said, "Well sir, that's about the prettiest thing I've seen in quite a while. What do you think, Martin?"

"Sheriff, folks, I've never seen gold this pure come straight out of the ground so this is new for me. That is why I had trouble believing you last week, Juan. It doesn't seem to be petering out either way so you're going to have to be very careful in digging. You might even want to contact a mining geologist/engineer to help you with how to proceed. Just looking at what we can see, if it is only an inch thick, you're looking at several hundred thousand dollars' worth and you have hardly even begun to dig. Juan, you and Bernice have some deciding to do."

"Ok folks, I've seen enough," the Sheriff said, "if you're ready, let's find the sunshine." With Juan leading, the party hiked back to the entrance and the warmth of day.

Then the Sheriff continued, "Juan, I don't know what you got in mind, but if you ran into town and started celebrating, this whole hillside would be crawling with gold-diggers by morning. Now it's my job to keep the peace in this area and I could use your cooperation in the next few days."

"Sheriff, there's nothing I'd like better than taking your advice on how to proceed."

"Well sir, I'd recommend having Martin send for that geologist feller, and you folks fence in your whole spread. Martin, they're going to have to turn some of this gold into money right away to upgrade their place. What's the right way to do that?"

"Bring it down to me, some every day if you want. I'll test it and pass it on to Manning at the bank and he will credit your account accordingly. We could do it that way for quite a while without causing too much of a hullabaloo, Juan, that is if you folks want to keep a lid on this thing."

"Yes sir. I have some down at the house I'll send with you to get things started. And Sheriff, I'll send an order for fencing with you to hand to Gates at the hardware store, if you will, and we'll get to fencing, pronto."

When the two big horses and their riders had left, Juan and Bernice sat out on the porch and talked and planned as best they could. They were feeling wonderfully at peace, not feeling the need to shout from the mountain top.

Evening brought dinner and more family fun and planning for the next few days. Tomorrow would be early morning digging, followed by a trip into town. Family prayers that night were filled with thanksgiving and a plea for continued guidance.

As covers were pulled up to their chins, Juan asked Bernice if she thought God had put that gold there recently or if it had been there for millions of years. Before she had formed an answer, the long day caught up with them. They both fell peacefully asleep.

12

Loads of work went into the upgrading of Juan's ranch. A new entrance gate with the family name, and strong fencing all around the perimeter, gave a look of permanence to the place. All this was provided by Gates at the Hardware store, through Manning at the bank, by a good word from the Sheriff that was short on detail but long on confidence.

The geologist/engineer came and recommended shoring the mine from start to end with heavy timbers because of the random earthquakes. Loads of work to do, but fun because the gold was there.

Juan now knew he could count on God no matter what the circumstances were. His performance based on his experience in working with God had showed him that. Wasn't that what faith was?

Early every morning Juan went up and dug enough gold to fill a saddle bag, and every other day he rode into town and dropped two saddle bags worth off at Martin's office. He made sure he stopped at the hardware store and picked up something. He spoke, acted, and tried to think normally.

So far, no more earthquakes, and the shoring was proceeding. They had hired two of Bernice's younger brothers who needed work. They respected their older sister and were not told why the work was necessary. Better to keep things in the family where explanations could be kept to a minimum.

Juan was not going to dig away more rock until the shoring was to the end. He was oh so careful when he dug the gold each morning. Silently, reverently, he worked as if the mine was sacred. With prayer and care, he worked the mine. His humble attitude held back the force of the curse. That was his part. God, of course, was doing His job, plus keeping a careful eye on Juan's character development.

As weeks passed, Juan's thinking about this slowly changed. He had thought his part was vital in order to jump start God into doing His part, and his ongoing performance was vital to God's ongoing blessing. Now he began to wonder if he didn't have that backwards. Maybe it was God's performance that jumped started him. If the gold had been there for a long time, God had already done His part. Juan's work was just a way of receiving what God had already provided. He had never seen it that way before. Could it be that God wanted him and his family to enjoy the benefits of the gold so earnestly, that He drew Juan to a mine with pure gold in it, and put in his heart the will to dig? Perhaps simply believing that God wanted him to have the gold, and that gold was actually there, would have made his years of digging a lot less stressful and a lot more fun.

But what about his character development? Wasn't the blessing related to how well he did?

One morning, Juan woke up and realized he had dreamt the same dream as before: the dream where his part was effortless. He went through the routine of the day thinking about it. In the evening, after dinner, after the kids were in bed, and with Bernice by his side in front of the dying fire, his thoughts had boiled down to simplicity.

Juan spoke out loud, but softly, "The assurance of the gold being there, makes the work fun, not hard." He was still working, but he enjoyed and looked forward to it every day, thus the effortlessness on his part. "What if I would have had the assurance that the gold was there before I had actually seen it?" Is that what faith was? He would think more about this.

Bernice whispered as they headed for bed, "Thank you for choosing me for your wife."

Juan looked at her and smiled, "You're welcome. I'm glad I did."

That day changed things for Juan. He was experiencing riches from God, even though he had only stumbled into it. Had God actually been leading him? If so, it seemed sort of superstitious as he looked back to think his performance was the measure of how much gold God wanted him to have. He began to think that God's part was a whole lot bigger and more vital than his part in this life he was living. Could God possibly want him to have more gold than he could imagine without it being tied to how he performed? His performance was still important, but not in relation to the amount of blessing God wanted him to have. Could that possibly be true?

Juan would see his neighbors in town who had mines like his up and down the valley. Had any of them struck gold like he had and were keeping it quiet, too? Surely he was not the only one. He began mingling with his neighbors more when he was in town. He tried to see if any of them were excited but purposely being vague, like him.

One guy was not hiding what he found. He was in the bar drinking and telling anyone who would listen about what he had found. But the man had a bit of a reputation as a scoundrel, and nobody believed him.

One afternoon, Juan dropped into the bar and sat close enough to hear what the scoundrel had to say. Some people roared with laughter, others felt sorry for him. Basically, no one wanted to be associated with him.

After a while, Juan sat down next to him and whispered, "I want to see what you've found."

The man looked up, stunned, "What do you mean?"

"Did you find gold in your mine?"

"Yes. It's the most beautiful thing I've ever seen. Would you like to see it?"

"Yes, but only if it is pure gold."

"What? Yes, it is…but no one believes me."

"I do."

"You do? Do you want to see it?"

"Yes, let's go right now."

"Ok, come on." The man got up too fast, but Juan helped him out of the bar and into his buggy. The air was sobering the man up fast, but while Juan drove, the man kept up a steady tale about the gold.

Juan realized something. The man's drinking and talking about what he found was just his way of dealing with the treasure. Juan's way was to be vague and careful because he was afraid of God's dealings with him, even though God knew what was best for him. But Juan would bet the scoundrel and he had found the same thing. So which was the best way to deal with it?

When the man pointed to the turn off to his mine, Juan realized they were neighbors. He had probably found the same vein Juan had. The two men got out of the buggy and lit lanterns and walked into the mine. Juan counted his steps as he followed the man. Sure enough, just before fifty feet they hit rubble blocking the way.

The man stopped and pointed. "There."

"I only see rubble."

"It was there, but the earthquake covered it up."

Juan shook his head slowly and smiled. He had gone through the same experience. "Did you see gold before the earthquake?"

"Yes, yes," the man said looking at Juan hoping someone would believe him. "I saw it. It was the prettiest thing I have ever seen. And nobody can make me change my mind."

"I believe you."

"You should have seen it…You do? You believe me?"

"Yes I do. Come on, I want to hear more about it." And Juan led the way out of the mine.

13

The shoring was now all the way to the gold. Juan began digging rock away and wheel-borrowing it to a spot where the brothers could meet him without seeing the gold. Their job was to wheel it out and dump it, carefully, looking for gold in the rubble. This kept them excited about coming to work and joining in the treasure hunting without knowing anything about what was already there.

Juan kept up his early morning gold digging, the late morning and early afternoon rubble digging, and his every other day trip into town in the later afternoon. Sometimes Bernice went with him, and sometimes the whole family. On the days they all stayed home, they worked together around the ranch and enjoyed each other.

There was a change happening, and Juan was just watching it happen. He knew his ability to be hyper-anxious and get as much gold out before the mine collapsed again, was real. What if the whole town found out and tried to kill him in order to get the gold? Then there was the need to invest what he was storing up and make it grow so when the gold came to an abrupt end he would have his money already working for him. Oh so many thoughts and ideas came to mind. And to ignore them was irresponsibility, stupidity, and neglect of his family. That is, it should be.

However, he couldn't get away from the fact that his heart was contented. He wasn't sure how that happened. The peace and joy and contentment were stronger than the anxiousness and fear. The work was enjoyable, not hard, and family time was relaxed. In fact, they had fun as a family, hearing about needy neighbors and figuring out how to help them, sometimes without the people knowing who had helped.

Juan and Bernice would think and talk about this. It wasn't the potential of finding gold that brought peace. It wasn't the digging that brought them joy, knowing that hard work might bring a reward. It wasn't the mounting accumulation that brought contentment. It was actually owning the gold mine that brought those wonderful things, and when he had taken possession of it years ago, he had just been minding his own business, not knowing for sure if putting the mine in his name was the right thing to do, or not.

The more they thought and talked, the more they simplified it down. The mine was in their name. The gold was in the mine, and God had put that gold there a long time ago. Their peace, joy, and contentment were a reality because God had put something very valuable, a long time ago, in their path. They had simply discovered it, and were discovering more every day.

Actually, the whole valley was benefiting from Juan's gold mine, even though he and Bernice weren't always aware of it. Their calm countenance and do-gooding was silently affecting the whole town. It was like a lovely perfume that brought a whiff of pleasantness, even though nobody quite knew who was wearing it.

One family, living content and secure, because of the gold, had an influence on others even though others had not found gold. And the family was not talking wildly about the gold they had found. They just lived the peace and joy the gold brought to them.

They didn't tell others to work harder and dig deeper in their own mines, because gold really was there. Instead, they shared what they had. Not just the gold, but the affect it had on them. The family daily harvested the gold, and enjoyed it, and shared the richness with others.

What about the curse? Where was it? Good question. Maybe it had disappeared the moment the gold had been uncovered. Maybe it was the gold that satisfied the anger of the curse.

Juan knew that neither he nor Bernice, nor their family, nor anyone in the whole valley deserved the good affect the gold was having on everyone. But it had shown up, in a mine that he inherited from a relative, and he had the legal right to harvest as much as he wanted and enjoy it. That was it. That was his part. The rest was just the affect God was having on everyone because of what He had done a long time ago.

And God, somehow, seemed to be pleased that Juan and Bernice and their family were enjoying it.

Why would God so richly bless Juan and his family?

Somehow, despite all his hard work and balance, and then his change of heart and mind, Juan still didn't feel he deserved it.

And it was true, he didn't.